# Life is a Near Death Experience

Skills for Illness, Aging, Dying, and Loss

---

Ajahn Sona

Birken Publications

Copyright © 2021 Ajahn Sona
Birken Forest Buddhist Monastery
birken.ca

All rights reserved.

ISBN: 9798503933680

"Whether 'tis nobler in the mind to suffer

The slings and arrows of outrageous fortune,

Or to take arms against a sea of troubles,

And by opposing end them."

---

~ *Hamlet* by William Shakespeare

# CONTENTS

|  | Acknowledgements | i |
|---|---|---|
|  | Introduction | iii |
| Part I | The Nature to Sicken | 1 |
|  | *Reflecting vs. Thinking* | 3 |
|  | *A Wise Response* | 4 |
|  | *Not News* | 7 |
|  | *The Voice of Another* | 10 |
|  | *Ways to Reduce Pain* | 13 |
|  | *Handful of Teachings: Part I* | 16 |
| Part II | How the Wise See Illness | 19 |
| Part III | The Big Picture | 39 |
|  | *The Buddha and The King* | 40 |
|  | *Don't Worry, Everything is Out of Control* | 42 |
|  | *Rehearsing for Death* | 45 |
|  | *Grand Truths* | 50 |
|  | *Your Constant Companion* | 55 |
|  | *Handful of Teachings: Part II* | 57 |
|  | References/Glossary | 59 |
|  | About the Author | 61 |

# ACKNOWLEDGMENTS

Even though this book is small in stature, many hours and days of wholesome efforts have been expended by several people to bring this publication to the world. I wish to express gratitude to Upasika Piyadassi, Upasika Bodhipala, and Upasika Sumana for editing and designing the book.

May you all share in the great merit of their work.

Ajahn Sona<br>
Birken Forest Buddhist Monastery<br>
British Columbia, Canada

# INTRODUCTION

The theme of this small book is illness and how to reduce the emotional suffering that can occur in its presence. We are not passively subject to experience illness with fear, anxiety or depression. We can make choices about how we react to illness, and the prospect of death.

The first section of the book is likely to have wide appeal and be useful to a general audience. The last section of the book gives a Buddhist context for the large view of reality. If the first section helps you, that is all that matters. If you are curious about the Buddhist view of things, the second section may be of interest.

May you be well,<br>
Ajahn Sona

# PART I:

# THE NATURE TO SICKEN

*I am of the nature to age; I have not gone beyond aging.*

*I am of the nature to sicken; I have not gone beyond sickness.*

*I am of the nature to die; I have not gone beyond dying.*

*All that is mine, beloved and pleasing, will become otherwise, will become separated from me.*

*I am the owner of my kamma, heir to my kamma, born of my kamma, related to my kamma, abide supported by my kamma; whatever kamma I shall do, for good or for ill, of that I will be the heir.*

*Thus we should frequently recollect.*

*~ Five Subjects for Frequent Recollection* [1]

---

[1] AN 5.57: Abhinhapaccavekkhitabbathanasutta (Five Subjects for Frequent Recollection)

The very fact that you're reading this little book means you are looking for answers, answers to help you feel better in the midst of sickness, and perhaps in all areas of your life; ways to look at and address the general disease that follows us all around, every moment of every day. But before we start to explore the answers, I'd like to ask you a question: when is the best time to think about being sick?

Is it when you start to feel not so great? Perhaps when you first learn of your diagnosis? On your way to the hospital? Or is it, maybe, long before then? Could it be that the best time to contemplate illness, and even death, is when you're feeling healthy and have no cares in the world?

Let's begin with a very basic truth: we are all subject to illness. At first glance this statement seems obvious, and yet, when a serious illness arises in ourselves or our loved ones, many of us are blindsided by this existential fact of life. Even if you reach the end of your life having never been ill, it *could* have happened. So, most of the time people put it out of their minds completely. They don't like to think about it, and in some ways that's not a bad approach. But when they do finally think about it, the possibility of having a serious or terminal disease, that prospect can make them nervous, anxious, fearful, depressed. And if that's the case, putting it aside hasn't worked very well.

What the Buddha suggests instead is to reflect on this possibility through the Five Subjects for Frequent Recollection. Five subjects, easy to remember on just one hand. The first one is that human beings are of the nature to age; second, we can get ill; third is that we all will die; fourth, we'll lose everything we love along the way; and the last one is that whatever we do, whether it's good or bad, we are responsible for that outcome. And these reflections are to be done not just once in a while, but many times throughout the day. In fact, it's much better if you contemplate these long before you get sick.

## Reflecting vs. Thinking

It's important to realize that reflecting is quite different from thinking. Reflecting on illness and recollecting the possibility of being sick and dying is done in an entirely different spirit than just thinking about it happening. The atmosphere of your mind must not be tainted by anxiety and fear. We want to process this information when we're in the right mood, from a place of tranquility and ease. Can you realize that you're vulnerable, subject to sickness, and that sickness can lead to death, without these realities depressing you or causing you anxiety? Now, that would be a good state of mind to be in, because it's the real situation.

This is a core tenet of Buddhism: that you can actually look at these stark truths about what it is to be a ve, vulnerable human being, without experiencing the negative emotions that typically accompany us through life. This is a radically different way of looking at these things. You can really and truly walk around in this world - in touch with reality - and *still* be okay.

Shock-proofing your life by staying in touch with these realities all the time is the first strategy for reducing suffering and increasing your resiliency. The Buddha asks us to do the opposite of what the mind wants to do. In the face of illness, death and loss, our standard operating procedure is to seek certainty and security. That's a basic mistake. To feel at ease only when you feel secure and stable is a big mistake. We actually have to reverse the operations of our mind and remind ourselves every day, many times throughout the day, that it's never, ever secure, it's never fully safe: that is the fact.

### A Wise Response

Once we are familiar with the Five Frequent Recollections, we can then take the next step in our reflections: what is an intelligent emotional response to this situation? The Buddha says it's not wishing it was some other way, not being surprised or horrified by it, nor refusing to think about it. It's to see that you have a choice: you can suffer or not. I suggest you take door number two: choose not to suffer.

Instead of retreating into regret, worry, despair or fear, we really want to turn towards a way out of suffering, towards another way of being. Equanimity, loving-kindness, compassion, but no fear. You rehearse these attitudes until they become second nature. You bring them up at the same time as you're relaxing, and you'll start feeling at ease in the midst of this absolute insecurity and uncertainty.

And this practice isn't just done while meditating. You can be walking around and doing your chores, driving to work, cooking dinner, functioning and interacting with people, living all the time within a healthy mindset.

In contrast, quite often the standard dialogue around illness and death is fanned by the flames of heightened drama: a sense of the tragedy, the fearfulness, how unfair it all is. It's not uncommon for the ordinary person, or even people who should know better, like health professionals and psychologists, to demand that you be in a state of fear, worry or depression over such things. If you're not, they may even pull out this dire pronouncement: "Denial!" They will tell you, most emphatically, "You're in denial, you're not accepting it, otherwise you would be experiencing sadness about your predicament."

There was a woman I knew who had multiple sclerosis, and she was quite naturally philosophical about it. She was a mother with kids and a family. She was also a nurse, and then she got this disease. The symptoms began and it was really progressing quickly. Her doctor eventually suggested she see a psychiatrist because she seemed to be in denial. Now, I learned about this because her mother, a regular visitor to Birken, had brought her here to the monastery. We were amazed. She was in a wheelchair by this time, and she was remarkably Buddhist about it. She was not at all in fear about her situation.

So, she went to the psychiatrist as her doctor requested. The psychiatrist talked to her and the woman calmly said, "What am I supposed to be afraid of? I work as a nurse. I know that people die. Don't you? What do you think I'm in denial of? Do you think I should be sad or upset about this?"

In the end, the psychiatrist actually agreed with her and phoned her doctor to say, "You sent your patient to me thinking that there's something terribly wrong with her, that she should be overcome with grief and have a big problem about this illness. Yet I find that she's responding in an enlightened, philosophical fashion while you're saying she's in denial. Doctor, I think maybe *you* are the one who is in denial!"

The doctor's shallow judgement is the mark of a lack of wisdom, and it's pervasive throughout the modern world. It's a lack of wisdom, ignorance really, to say things like that. It is actually possible for people who have some wisdom to face situations like death and illness without fear, without sadness. As Buddhists, we aspire to that wise attitude.

## Not News

When you're ill, you need supportive voices, voices which encourage the idea that you should not slip into this type of tragic drama. If you don't have them, you're likely to be misdirected constantly by other people: family members, friends, and professionals like doctors and psychologists. It's very likely that you're going to have a voice or even many voices of misdirection strongly suggesting that this is a very scary emergency you're going through. You may even receive a phone call one day that goes something like this: "Unfortunately I have some bad news. I want you to come in as soon as possible."

"I have bad news." Right off the bat they're already telling you two incorrect things: that this is bad and that it's news. Wrong, wrong, wrong!

Well, here is my news: it's not news. It can't really be bad news or good news because it's not news at all. There's nothing new about it. This is what we're reminding ourselves of again and again when we contemplate the second of those Five Subjects for Frequent Recollection: "I am of the nature to sicken; I have not gone beyond sickness."

That nature is activated when you come into the world. The very day you were born you acquired the potential for disease, whether it be from a coronavirus or cancer or AIDS or a heart attack or a stroke, or any of the thousands of illnesses that could end your life. There's nothing surprising or new about this information. Wise, resilient people don't live with their heads in the sand, wishing or hoping that it won't happen. When illness appears, they don't ask, "Why me?" Instead, they say, "Why *not* me? "

Illness should never be surprising. Good and bad are merely suggestions to your emotional psyche. In contrast, the wise response is knowing it is not helpful to fall into negative emotions while you or a loved one are sick.

Even to call it "your" body is a mistake. It's not "your" body. This thing grows by itself and is the product of complex biological laws. It's essentially just borrowed, a loaner vehicle, if you will, from Mother Nature. It's not something that is you or yours, and it never was. Anybody who thinks about that for even a few minutes realizes this truth.

We confuse ourselves by talking about it as "our" body. And if it was your body, you wouldn't, for example, have COVID-19 now would you? Yet the coronavirus or some other illness has shown up in this borrowed vehicle called "the body". This is very important. This is not just an interesting philosophical idea. This is extraordinarily important, because when it's your illness, there are things to be afraid of. When it's *not* your illness, there's *nothing* to be afraid of.

Consider this: the phone rings and someone on the other end says, "I have some bad news: you have cancer." The ordinary person feels deflated. They feel overwhelmed. They feel nervous, afraid, maybe even terrified. Then the phone rings again 20 minutes later and, with great apologies, the caller says, "Oh, I'm so sorry. We made a mistake. You don't have cancer. That was somebody else's report."

How do you feel now? You likely feel a great sense of relief. You might even laugh hysterically. You don't have cancer! Of course, somebody else you don't know does have it, but we celebrate that "I" don't have cancer. Notice the ownership issue here. When it's your cancer, it's a problem; when it's not your cancer: no problem.

Somebody's body has cancer, but it's not your problem. Think about that. When "you" have cancer, there's a big issue looming over "you"; but when "the body" has cancer, a body which is not *your* body, it's not an issue at all.

This may sound tricky or subtle. It's not. It's the obvious fact right in front of your face; no one can deny it. You don't own and control your body. It runs by itself, and therefore a sense of ownership and identity with your body should be abandoned. And the sooner, the better. It's very dangerous for you. When you have a strong sense of a false identification with your body, you are going to subject yourself over and over again to pain, to fear, to anxiety and despair. Reflecting on this truth will help you immensely, and it will relieve so many areas of suffering in your life.

## The Voice of Another

When illness does arise, your friends and family are going to be talking to you about it, and you might be attending counselling groups, listening to other people who have the same disease or other illnesses. All of these people are going to be in deluded states of confusion and turmoil.

I mentioned in the previous section that you need supportive voices at this time, not those of misdirection, leading you into unnecessary states of dramas. The first blessing the Buddha offers in The Great Discourse on Blessings[2] is not to associate with the foolish; the second blessing is to associate with the wise. What this means is that you must try to avoid people who talk about fear or anger, or people who bring up emotions of anxiety with their advice to you.

---

[2] KP 5: Mangalasutta (The Great Discourse on Blessings)

The other way to encounter unwise voices is by listening to certain media or reading things that make you feel afraid, anxious or depressed. Much of today's media will try to pull you into its pervasive drama by creating fear and worry, because it exists to catch your attention. If you buy into any of these foolish influences, you might start forgetting that it is not your body. You really can't afford to associate with these people, with any negative media or negative fiction, especially now that you have this illness.

On the flip side is the wise voice of another, my voice or somebody else's voice talking in the same mode, which can quickly and effectively pull you out of your false sense of identity with your body, and the suffering which accompanies that kind of unwise thinking. Have some resources on hand, this book or other related books, video or audio recordings, that you read or listen to on a regular basis. These wise voices will pull you out of wrong ideas about your body and about how to respond to this illness.

This is very, very important. The Buddha himself says the voice of another can be profoundly helpful to you, but that voice has to be the voice of wisdom. It can't be the voice of folly. You can't expect your neighbor or your friends or your family to necessarily be wise about these things. They're going to have all kinds of inadequate responses. Perhaps they're wise; how fortunate it would be if they were! But you have to make sure, because it's so important that you listen to wise voices, not unwise ones.

How will you know the difference? The mark of a wise voice is that, after listening to it, you actually feel better. You feel less afraid. You feel less anxious. You feel well and happy and peaceful, but in touch with the truth at the same time.

And the truth is that this body is a product of nature and the process of all illness is natural; it naturally happens. It's not something unnatural, it's not something that shouldn't happen. As I said earlier, it's not bad news; it's not news at all. It's just the nature of the body to get ill. It is truly that simple.

So search out those voices of wisdom that pull you into a state of uplifting ease, of well-being, of loving-kindness. Find the voice of another, whether it be in a book or a magazine you're reading, in a talk you're listening to, in a video you're watching. It doesn't matter whether it's a fictional work or a fact-based one. If you're not able to generate this yourself, put on your headphones, lie in bed, lie in a hammock, sit, go for a walk, whatever you have to do, and truly experience the voice of another pulling you out of any unwise state. If it has to be this very book, very good. Read it, listen to it, absorb those wise words into every cell of your being, again and again and again.

## Ways to Reduce Pain

Now we need to have some strategies for dealing with pain as well. Pain may come up. The first thing to know is that pain is one feeling, and the fear of pain is another. It's important to remember that the fear of pain is far worse than the actual pain. So, since we might have physical pain, we should be very, very determined not to make it any worse. That means that you can't afford to be afraid of it. You can't afford to worry about it, to be anxious about it, to hope that you won't experience it. Instead, you need to put it firmly in its place: pain is simply a bodily sensation.

It's not that we want to just "face the pain." There's no heroism in this. If you get medications which reduce the pain, by all means take them. But sometimes they only dull the pain and then you need some strategies to help reduce the high awareness of bodily pain.

First and foremost, what you need to do is put your mind on something else other than the pain. Reframing the experience is essential, but it matters which frame you use, how you shift your perception of the situation. Some people will tell you to just go into the pain. This is not necessarily good advice. It is far better to put your mind on an object which *replaces* the object of pain. You have to strongly go to some other sensation or thought, and you have to invest in it very deeply. The Buddha himself had pain in his back and he said, "The only time I'm free of pain is when I'm in *jhana*. When I'm in deep *samadhi*, meditation, I don't feel the pain."

This is the essence of meditation. It is a reframing of the world, a reframing of our thoughts and feelings around it. It really helps if you have practiced this ahead of time, but, if you haven't, this is as good a time as any to start.

I want to suggest two different objects that you can fully immerse your mind in to get free of this sensation called pain. If you give your wholehearted attention to them, it's possible that pain will be so far away from your awareness that you won't actually experience it for periods of time.

The first object is the breath: the simple experience of air entering the body in the nasal cavity and exiting the body through the nasal cavity. This nasal cavity is a spacious area inside your head. I'm not necessarily talking about the medical or biological nasal cavity, but the one you *feel*. It's the airy, spacious quality inside your head. When you breathe in, the air is usually cooler. When you breathe out, it's about body temperature.

Place all your attention on that light and airy space in the nasal cavity and you will feel like your head is full of air. This is a lovely place to go and spend as long as you want there. It's a tremendous way of reducing the experience of pain, but it won't happen if you are doubtful about it. You need to be confident, and fully and wholeheartedly immerse yourself in that lovely, light, cool air. You can help keep the mind attentive by counting: count the out breaths from one up to five and then start again at one. If you lose your place, come back to one and keep counting the breaths from one to five. This will be a great pain reliever.

The second object to turn your attention to is loving-kindness. When you have placed your mind fully on loving-kindness, there is no room for fear, dread, sorrow, any of those negative emotions. They are mutually exclusive. When you're experiencing loving-kindness, you feel safe, and this has a great ability to reduce pain in the body. Unlike any other thing you can imagine, a true felt sense of loving-kindness gives you freedom from fear: fear of pain, fear of the future, fear of the past, fear of death, all of these unnecessary burdens. Fear goes away, and that's what you want. You have released yourself from fear, and this is profound.

Now, loving-kindness is not something you just practice randomly. As you move through your day, look for, bring up, and find objects of loving-kindness that naturally draw you into this warm emotion. For some people it's kittens, puppies, children, babies, grandmothers, grandfathers, parents, or friends. Choose whoever or whatever is easy. This is not a challenging exercise. You're in no situation to be challenged. You need things that are easy to love, and you're going to just immerse yourself in them. If you absorb yourself in this practice, preoccupy yourself with this, fill yourself with this all day long, pain will naturally diminish and recede into the distance.

---

# Handful of Teachings: Part 1

*Reflecting vs. Thinking:* Contemplate the Five Subjects for Frequent Recollection (I'm of the nature to age, to sicken, to die, to lose everything I love, and I am responsible for all my actions and the outcomes of those actions) over and over again until they are running seamlessly in your mind all day and all night.

*A Wise Response:* If regret, worry, despair or fear, come up for you, replace those negative emotions as quickly as you can with positive ones. Cultivate the proper responses of joy, ease, equanimity, loving-kindness, compassion, and fearlessness.

*Not News:* Illness should never be a surprise, and it's certainly not news. Good and bad are just habitual suggestions to your mental framework. Remember that it's not your body, it's not your illness. It is merely a process that started its journey the day you were born.

***The Voice of Another:*** Avoid foolish voices and messages that attempt to stir up negative thoughts and emotions for you. Seek out only the voice of the wise, whether found in books, magazines, audio recordings, videos, or Dhamma talks. This wise voice is your new best friend.

***Ways to Reduce Pain:*** Begin or deepen a practice of meditation. Two simple objects are the breath and loving-kindness. Through meditation you are strengthening a new pathway for your mind, away from pain and towards only positive emotions. Just these two meditation subjects can serve you exceedingly well in all stages of your life.

## PART II:

# HOW THE WISE SEE ILLNESS

*We are what we think.*
*All that we are arises with our thoughts.*
*With our thoughts we make the world.*
*Speak or act with an impure mind*
*And trouble will follow you*
*As the wheel follows the ox that draws the cart.*

*We are what we think.*
*All that we are arises with our thoughts.*
*With our thoughts we make the world.*
*Speak or act with a pure mind*
*And happiness will follow you*
*As your shadow, unshakable.* [3]

---

[3] Dhammapada v. 1-2

We've just explored a number of techniques that can change your approach to illness; a practical checklist of things to remember, do, and reflect upon throughout your day. Ideally you will have put in the time and effort long before you become seriously ill to practice, hone, and refine these skills. Yet, as we now know, illness and pain can arise at any moment, often without warning.

What follows is a conversation I had with Upasika Piyadassi, a laywoman who has served as our office steward for a number of years here at Birken Monastery, after she went through the experience of cancer.

The guidance and strategies we discuss can be applied to any disease, from chronic pain to terminal illness, or even the common cold. Having these skill sets ready in your emotional toolbox will be a great gift to yourself throughout your life, and most especially as you near the end of life.

---

*Ajahn Sona:* How the wise see cancer is our topic. I hope this is helpful and useful in some way for anybody dealing with cancer personally, or for somebody else you may know who has cancer. Of course, it's not just cancer; it's any serious illness. The Buddha and Buddhism have a lot to offer in how to view the experience of sickness and its universal potential for any human being.

For most humans, one day they will be sick, and that illness can terminate in death or in recovery. We need strategies, we need attitudes, we need the right view of things to deal with this and to minimize suffering. There is physical pain, and then there's emotional distress. The area that we're going to work with the most is how to reduce emotional suffering as much as possible. Of course, if you can also reduce the physical suffering, that would be wonderful as well.

So we're going to talk to Upasika Piyadassi, our lovely office steward at Birken Monastery, and a long-term practitioner. I'm talking to her because she had cancer and we had to work through this together. I want to find out from her what worked, what helped, what attitudes she turned to, and what she learned from the experience.

Let's just go back to your first awareness of symptoms, when you knew that something was wrong. Tell me about that.

*Upasika Piyadassi:* Ajahn, I was having some mucusy discharge that wasn't explainable. At that time, I was seeing an acupuncturist on a pretty regular basis, so on my next visit I told her of my symptoms and she took my pulses. She suggested I go for a colonoscopy, as well as get a stool sample. I did that and the results from the stool sample came back indicating they had found traces of blood. Not long after that I had a colonoscopy, and about a week later I got a call from my doctor's office to arrange for an MRI, which was my clue that something wasn't quite right. And, as I was talking to the nurse, the doctor got on the phone. Now when the doctor gets on the phone, again, that's not an optimistic prospect. He said, "Well, this isn't good news, and I prefer to tell you in person." That's when I knew for sure that this was not something positive.

I actually had an interview set with you that day, Ajahn, about some other matter. I went in to see you, and began to talk about what had happened with the doctor, and then I realized I had started to cry. I was kind of surprised that I was crying because I had already been sitting with this and mulling it over for about two hours.

I remember saying to you that I wasn't so afraid of dying, but I wanted liberation before I go. You said, "It starts now. You stay on the breath."

We talked a bit more about the idea that this was not news. You reminded me that, in fact, I didn't know what the news was yet; only that it wasn't good news. You encouraged me not to think about it because there was nothing else I could do at that point. I found that very helpful. I decided to get right to your suggestion about the breath, so I went to our meditation hall and started meditating. I remember feeling such gratitude that I was living at the monastery at a time when I was faced with this kind of prognosis and the future ahead of me, all of it completely unknown.

***Ajahn Sona:*** Now, you said I told you not to think about it. This is important. The first thing most people do when they hear they may have a serious illness, or even suspect it, is to start thinking about it - a lot. But these thought processes are not just useless, but extremely problematic because they usually bring up a whole bunch of anxiety and fear. The reason why I told you not to think about it is because people introduce all kinds of other illnesses into their experience, on top of the one they already have. The other illnesses are emotional ones. So the first thing I recommend is to very confidently understand the value of *not* thinking about it.

This is strange advice. Everybody else out there is saying, "Yes, you've got to think about it, and think about this, and think about that too." Nobody would suggest not thinking about it. But I'm suggesting exactly that! By the way, this is also the same advice I give to people who wake up in the middle of the night and worry about their problems in life. I tell them, "Never think at night." If you're going to think at all, it has to be in a state of ease, supported, rested, and with clarity. There is no value in thinking about such things when you are not at your best.

So this was good advice, and it helped you to decide on a strategy?

*Upasika Piyadassi:* Yes, it did, Ajahn. I ended up going the next day to see the doctor for the news. I was feeling very balanced because at that point I already had the understanding that something was not right. But I was also very much at peace, and I was just preparing myself to hear whatever had to be said.

The doctor told me that I had anal cancer. It was early stage as far as they could tell, but he was suggesting a treatment of chemo and radiation for six weeks and they would get that scheduled. I came back to the monastery and shared that information with you. I remember we discussed and processed those details together, both the illness and its treatment. I had wonderful support here.

*Ajahn Sona:* What does wonderful support look like?

*Upasika Piyadassi:* The first support was from you, saying that you were going to send me *metta* zaps!

*Ajahn Sona:* That's important and a nice strategy to suggest when other people ask what they can do for you. People will empathize with your pain, and they'll be full of all kinds of ideas about how they're going to help you. Sometimes those ideas are not that great. But you can always respond by asking them to think about you with loving-kindness. Loving-kindness doesn't mean, "I'm sad for you"; it means "May you be well, happy, and peaceful." When they bring you to mind, or any other person with an illness, ask them to visualize that person and radiate towards them this sentiment: "May you be well, may you be happy, may you be peaceful." It's nice to know that people are thinking about you in a very positive way.

I called it "zaps" because you were about to go and get zapped by radiation. *Metta*, loving-kindness, is a kind of radiation as well, radiating *metta*. I think you were a little apprehensive about this radiation that they were going to do at the cancer clinic. So that was one of our strategies: that you felt it was helpful to know people were going to do *metta* zaps for you on a regular basis, and that you would perhaps actually benefit from them as well. To know that people are doing it is one clear benefit, and then the power of those *metta* zaps is another.

So continue the story. Then what happened?

**Upasika Piyadassi:** I saw the doctor in mid-February, so it was the end of March when I was heading off for treatment. As you know, we have a belief in *kamma* and that both our good and unwholesome actions have fruit or consequences. It just so happened that a long-term guest arrived at Birken about that time. After I had seen my radiologist and received a second confirmation of the diagnosis, that very day, this kind guest said, "If I can fill in for you, I will do that while you're away."

That had been my main concern: how to take care of my duties here at the monastery while being away for six weeks of chemo and radiation. And the solution just manifested. I didn't ask and someone offered this spontaneously and generously. It brought up such gladness and *metta*, emotions that I could then radiate to other people. That made me feel better as well. So the good actions of the past perhaps brought this event forward that someone could help me just when I needed it. And there's another thing. I also felt that perhaps my previous unwholesome action was coming to fruition through the cancer and I rejoiced in that too: "Oh good, that one's paid off!"

***Ajahn Sona:*** So this needs to be explained, I think, especially for non-Buddhists. The idea is that we have all done negative and positive things in the past. First of all, to actually be a human at all means that you have done good things. To be born as a human is quite a remarkable achievement. Many people think it is just an accident of biology. Buddhists don't. The fact that you're human and that you have your faculties, your senses, means that you have done good things in the past. But then things happen to you in this life. Some of it is mysterious, but it has causes in the past, and we don't know specifically what those were. We just know that when negative things happen, that they are likely the results from previous negative causes.

The good side of this is that when you experience negative things, you're discharging a kind of debt. For example, when you stub your toe, you think, "Okay, one more debt paid off." Now, to be clear, you can't do this in a proactive way. You can't inflict pain on yourself in order to discharge debt. That's a bad idea. It's just something that happens to us from time to time: illnesses and difficulties and obstacles, but in order to turn that into a positive thing, you realize that it's one more negative thing paid off. This is one way of thinking about these things that is quite uplifting and can be very helpful.

*Upasika Piyadassi:* I also found it helpful that you recommended following the doctors' advice; just make it simple in that sense.

*Ajahn Sona:* Right. Buddhism doesn't have an issue with medical treatment. We're happy to cooperate. The Buddha himself had a personal physician and was quite happy to use the knowledge available to the world at that time. When it comes to medicine, Buddhists don't hold the belief that we'll only deal with illness in a purely spiritual way. Medicine can work, and there is a whole element of spiritual and psychological support as well.

*Upasika Piyadassi:* Ajahn, perhaps it was the practice at that point, but if you had asked me even earlier that year, "What would you do if you got cancer?", I might have said I'd look into alternative treatments and try all kinds of different approaches. But once I had cancer, I thought, I don't want to boggle my mind with making other decisions in that regard. It felt so good to let go of my views and opinions about finding the absolute, perfect, right thing to do. I had a good doctor; in fact, I was referred to a doctor who comes to the monastery, who is a Buddhist, and he took me on as a patient. As he was my oncologist, I felt totally at ease in following his advice, to go with Western medicine's approach to this disease.

That took a lot of weight off my mind, because what I also discovered was that as soon as you let people know you have a serious illness, their views and opinions start to flood in as to what you should do and what you shouldn't do, and I found that not at all helpful to my mindset. So to maintain my peace and to keep my mind in the game, so to speak, of the treatment regime I had chosen, I asked people not to share their views. I respected their opinions, but I had made a choice about my treatment and I was going to go forward in that decision with my full conviction.

*Ajahn Sona:* That's so important, to understand that you have a right, especially when you're sick, to not listen to other people. Not everybody's advice is helpful. You also have a right to just cut to the chase with others and say, "I'd rather not talk about it." There are all kinds of ideas in society about being open, receptive, talking about your inner pain and all those sorts of things. It's not necessarily helpful at all.

There are only certain people that you want to listen to, especially when you want a game plan or a helpful attitude because, generally speaking, people don't see cancer wisely. That's why the title of this little interview is "How the *Wise* See Cancer." Some of the advice that you're going to get about a wise approach to illness is very different from the ordinary approach. One recommendation is to stay away from discussions about this topic with most people, and just listen to your coach who is giving you the game plan. And this is a strategy not just for illness, but for all of life.

So then you went to the cancer clinic because you had to do the treatment, and it's full of other cancer patients, isn't it? Tell us a little bit about your strategies. How did you deal with the many different people and attitudes you encountered?

***Upasika Piyadassi:*** Well, my treatment was for six weeks of radiation, five days a week, and I was taking chemo every day as well, so I needed to relocate to Kelowna for that time and go to the BC Cancer Agency. Fortunately, they have a living facility right next door and, quite generously, friends offered to sponsor my stay there. But I had a roommate, we had meals every day with other cancer patients and their families. We would then walk over each day for our treatments. That was my living situation for six weeks.

Before I left the monastery, I also told people I was treating this time away as a retreat. I didn't want to hang out, although people offered. "Should I come and be with you, do you want to talk, should we go shopping, go for lunch?" I said, I really appreciate that, but I just want this to be an internal time for practice.

I told my roommate that as well, and she was very respectful of my wishes. But you'd be at a meal and the same questions would come up. Maybe the best analogy is of being in prison and the other inmates asking about your prison sentence: "What are you in for? What kind of cancer do you have? How long are you here for treatment?"

I remember early on when these types of questions came up, I would simply reply, "I have a lot of compassion for you, but I'd really rather not talk about my illness." I told them, "I'm just going to focus on being here and doing my treatment." I got some very odd looks, but they respected my boundaries, and I just kept my head down for meals. I would go for walks and basically kept to myself.

***Ajahn Sona:*** You and I had decided that you would essentially model this experience on a meditation retreat. At such a retreat, there are other people around and you're not unfriendly, but silence is the norm. You have your own life work to do, and you can't do everybody else's work as well. You can't just lay yourself out as a social being all the time. There's inner work that nobody else can do for you, and that you need to do by yourself, in silence.

Now those of you who have never been to a retreat might think that when you feel nervous, it's reassuring to have people talking to you. But I would suggest that there is greater value in keeping your own counsel or the counsel of the wise. It's not that you don't listen to other voices, but that you are very selective about them, so that you don't get pulled into unwanted confusion.

So, did you listen to any Dhamma talks?

***Upasika Piyadassi:*** I did. I watched some of your YouTube talks, and there were other Dhamma talks I had downloaded. I remember Bhikkhu Bodhi had a series on the *paramis,* perfections of character, and I listened to one of those each day. I also took one Dhamma book along. That was all I had, and I would read and meditate every day. I got up at 5:30 each morning so that I could mentally join the morning meditation at the monastery. I did that for the evening meditation session as well. As the treatment carried on, I found that I was very, very tired, and wasn't meditating as much as I wanted to. At that point I was sleeping quite a lot during the day.

More physical pain was starting to show up in the body, and my mind kept being drawn into that. One day I noticed my reflection in the mirror and my face had a grimace on it. At that moment I realized that I was anticipating pain, even though I was not feeling it at that moment. So I brought my awareness to that point: "Am I in pain now?" And if not, I reassessed my perception: "Oh good, there's no pain." When the pain returned, I brought my attention to seeing the arising and the passing of it, using meditation as much as I could to stay with the breath and find peace.

There was one particular time while sitting in meditation when the pain went away. It had been very intense, but I was meditating and the pain just disappeared. I felt such joy in realizing, "Oh, this meditation stuff really works."

*Ajahn Sona:* That's interesting. The capacity to center the mind in strong concentration can reduce pain. It's very important to know you have that option; that there is an alternative to pain if you can manage to focus your mind on a meditation object or on an object outside of oneself.

The way this works is that pain dissolves corresponding to the degree of concentration you have. Just to the degree that you're focusing on another object, pain in the background will diminish. It's like a teeter totter: focus on this end, the other end goes down. Now, not everybody has the capacity to concentrate like this, so you've got to confirm it for yourself, work with it, and learn, "Oh, this actually works."

***Upasika Piyadassi:*** Ajahn, you mentioned coaching. I was thinking of you as my cancer coach through the entire treatment because we emailed a few times and you generously spoke with me over Skype as well. That was really supportive and helped me tremendously.

***Ajahn Sona:*** That's great: a spiritual coach, a psychological coach, but not just *any* coach because not everybody has good recommendations. There are so many conventional approaches about how to cope with sickness and not all of them are good. You're going to have to sort through this: what are really good ideas and what are not.

This is too complex to completely and thoroughly explain here, but the basic premise is that suffering is not a good idea. We want to reduce the amount of emotional distress. There is no great value in it. We want to reduce emotional pain, and physical pain as well. These are the strong intentions we must keep focusing on, investigating and recognizing what it is that brings us into suffering, and how to stay away from it.

***Upasika Piyadassi:*** Another thing that would come up, and I think it's a common theme when people have cancer, is the idea of battling it and fighting it. I really didn't have that sense at all. It's what you've talked about: "This body isn't mine." I would think, "It's not *my* cancer, it's got nothing to do with me." I remember saying that to a few people and they would look at me rather strangely.

***Ajahn Sona:*** That's a great help, the idea that the body is not yours. The body itself is not yours and therefore the cancer itself is not yours. It's not I, it's not me, it's not mine. Illnesses are biological processes that are completely natural. They occur, and if they did occur it means that they're part of whatever environment we're in. So we have to not identify with these things. It's important, and you will get a lot of relief when you see that illness is not personal. There is illness in a body, but it is not me.

***Upasika Piyadassi:*** I also saw this disease as a great opportunity to practice for death, because you can get a cold and you're pretty sure you're going to get well, but if you get cancer you don't know what the outcome might be. They'll give you the odds, like a betting game! We have a 70-80% success rate with this treatment, and you might be in that percentage or, maybe not. I looked at it as a great gift: I may not have much time left.

I had this thought: this could be a dress rehearsal for death, or it could be closing night! You just don't know. What I do know is that I want to be at peace every moment that I'm alive. Even to this day when I think of having cancer I feel such gratitude for its appearance in my life. It was a tremendous opportunity to really turn the flame up on my practice, to work with that sense of preparing for death and finishing my spiritual work.

*Ajahn Sona:* We're using the idea of death as an incentive to live, and to live well. The certainty of death and the uncertainty of when it will happen can be used as a wholesome uplifting idea.

And this is practical whether you are the one with cancer or the doctor who's treating a cancer patient. Nobody actually knows who's going to die first. The doctor could step out into traffic and lose their life, while the cancer patient might live to be a hundred. Nobody knows in this game; it's beyond our comprehension and our control.

The fact of death is something that we should have known since we were children. It's part of the condition of being born: death comes along with birth. The important thing is that we don't need to be in a state of fear about it. We can process this in a positive way, so that it fills our existence with the possibility of how to be in this very uncertain, unstable, and painful existence without increasing that pain.

So now, here you are! And it's been how long?

*Upasika Piyadassi:* A little over two and a half years.

*Ajahn Sona:* And how are you?

*Upasika Piyadassi:* I'm very well.

*Ajahn Sona:* And what do the doctors say?

*Upasika Piyadassi:* I had follow-up appointments every month for six months after the treatment and they found no evidence of the cancer. I've had a few diagnostic tests since then and it's all clear; the colon is clear and the anal wall is clear. I will probably need follow-ups for a couple more years, but I feel great.

I remember coming back to the monastery after my treatment, and there was a period of intense healing with quite a bit of pain. At one point the pain faded. And then it came back again, and I thought, "There's pain? Oh right, I had cancer. I forgot. Right." And then, I just didn't think about it again.

*Ajahn Sona:* Now after all the treatment is over and you're feeling better, it's no time to stop practicing. You have to continue to do this inner work, to live moment to moment. You've been through it all and come out the other side with no evidence of cancer, but the game still goes on. The fact of death remains. It remains for all of us, and we always have to keep that in mind. It's not just, "Oh, I had a close call and now I'm going to live forever." We're all in the same situation, all the time, and the lessons that you learned and that were presented to you are still being absorbed and practiced.

***Upasika Piyadassi:*** I remember there was one time I was getting radiation near the end of my six weeks and the tech said, "You're always smiling. Why is that?" "Well," I said, "it's better than the alternative!" I would make myself smile many times when I was in pain because it's uplifting.

That's something to remember in our day-to-day lives because we all have bad days for a variety of emotional reasons, or we're just not feeling well. To smile, or to bring a positive thought to mind, or to have *metta* for ourselves or for someone else, I think that's important. And, yes, just to remember that this could be the last breath. It's a wonderful thing to bring to the practice.

***Ajahn Sona:*** You've pointed out another little tip: the idea of smiling when you have no authentic feeling of happiness. Smiling as a kind of a reminder. It goes backwards in the mental circuits and reminds you of other positive experiences outside of illness. People often think they have to be authentic. "Well, I've got cancer. What are you talking about, smiling? That's Pollyanna kind of stuff." It's not Pollyanna kind of stuff.

Consider this: most people have cancer before they know they have it, and they can be walking around, smiling and feeling no fear whatsoever. Then, they are told they have cancer. There's very little difference between the day when they didn't know and the day when they *do* know. So why not smile? You were smiling before you learned you had cancer, why don't you continue? In fact, it's *because* you have cancer that it's a good idea to smile.

I have a saying: "The worse it gets, the better I feel." That's a strange saying, but I'm going to leave it for you to contemplate and to unravel. I'm not going to explain why "The worse it gets, the better I feel" is a good thing to contemplate. Most people would say, "The worse it gets, the worse I feel; the better it gets, the better I feel." Actually, the reverse is very, very important: "The worse it is, the better you *must* feel."

Thank you, Piya, very much. The fact that you can share this experience with others is one of the benefits of having gone through the valley of death and come out the other side. Lots of people have to face illness, and that's why we're doing this little series on how the wise see cancer. We want to turn this into a positive thing and to share solid, Buddhist strategies for facing illness and all the other certain uncertainties of life.

# PART III:

# THE BIG PICTURE

*Know that the body is a fragile jar,*

*And make a castle of your mind.*

*In every trial*

*Let understanding fight for you*

*To defend what you have won.*[4]

---

[4] Dhammapada v. 40

## The Buddha and The King

About a year ago all of us first learned the name of a new disease: COVID-19. A litany of repurposed and original terms entered our vocabulary and our daily lives: social distancing, herd immunity, contact tracking, lockdown, forced isolation, mask-up, elbow bump. Since the pandemic's spread across the world, all aspects of our lives have shifted in one way or another. Some people think we're in an unusual time, a time of mass illness and death, but actually there's nothing unusual about this time at all.

That's why I keep repeating "illness, aging, death, loss", over and over and over again. It's a little like memorizing a poem or a recipe: you have to keep the words on the tip of your mind so they will be ready the moment you need them. The Buddha asks us to recollect this handful of five conditions every day, maybe four or five times a day, and really get to know these truths: that humans are of the nature to get ill, to age, to die, and to lose everything which we love along the way. That is constant. That's every day, every single moment of every single day; that is a fact of human existence. And then there's the last of the five, which is this: "My inheritance is my ethical decisions. What I have decided in life, what I have done for good or for ill, of that I will be the heir."

This is the case for all of us. Yet somehow, every now and then we get startled by these events.

In December 2004 there was a tsunami in Asia that hit Sri Lanka and Thailand and the coast of India. A quarter million people died in about an hour. It hit most people as a shock. We were in winter retreat at that time and I was asked to go to Vancouver. I remember looking forward to winter retreat, the solitude, etc., and then I got an email about this news. Then the news got worse and worse and worse.

At first they said a few thousand people; they were just counting the bodies they had found. The numbers trickled in, but eventually it became obvious it was a quarter million people at least. So the Thai and Sri Lankan communities got together in Vancouver and invited monks to do some blessings. Some of the survivors were there who had been in this tsunami, had been swept away by it, and had lived. They came up on stage and told their various stories, and then I was invited to give a Dhamma talk on this situation as well. Immediately what came to mind was that the tsunami was very similar to a story about the Buddha and a King.

In this story, the Buddha asks, "Oh great King. What if you hear that a wall of mountains, the size of the Himalayas, is rolling towards you from the north, towards the kingdom, and all living beings are crushed by it. No living being escapes. Then the same message comes from the south, then from the east, and then from the west. You're surrounded, oh King. No living being escapes." Then the Buddha asks, "What will you do?"

What are the first four of the Five Recollections? Illness, aging, death, loss. Those are the mountains as high as the Himalayas. So the King, being a good disciple of the Buddha, answers him, "I will do acts of charity and keep the precepts." That's the fifth and final reflection: "Whatever I do for good or for ill, that will be my inheritance."

## Don't Worry, Everything is Out of Control

The fact is that this kind of thing is going on all the time. What I mean by that is even when a tsunami or a pandemic like this happens, probably in the large statistical view of things, it won't make much difference to the mortality rate on the planet. Even at the longest, everybody on the planet, even the ones who were born today, everybody will be dead within about a hundred years, about a century.

So you consider the population of the planet, which is approaching eight billion people. Eight billion people have to die in the next hundred years and that's a lot of people. About 55 million people die on a regular basis every year from various things so the statistics won't wobble very much, even though you have this huge tsunami of COVID-19 deaths. We're always in this situation, but every now and then it seems the illusion of it being some sort of aberration comes up in people's minds and in the media. Buddhists should always be fully aware of this truth all the time.

All you've got to know is one thing: I was born. If you're born as a human, you have a predisposition to illness, a certainty of aging, and a certainty of death. If you are shocked by that or distressed by that, then you're in denial. And it just so happens that a pandemic is one of the things that makes a lot of people shocked and distressed.

Yet there's all kinds of ways to go. Cancer is an epidemic. Heart disease is an epidemic. So are opioid addiction and alcoholism. All of these are huge, widespread ailments, increasing in the population, so COVID-19 is just one of many dreadful possibilities for the human body. And the dreadful possibility is built in at birth. It's a dreadful possibility for the body, but it is not a dreadful possibility for the mind. Undoing this kind of thinking is what you need to do. As the Buddha says in the Dhammapada, "Know that the body is a fragile jar, and make a castle of your mind."

Another huge impact of this pandemic is that the economy will be severely shaken. Through this we're seeing loss, the fourth reflection, in a myriad of forms. Here's another thing about Buddhism: we're big on uncertainty, on the fact that you can't really know these things. There are all kinds of people predicting what will happen to the economy and what the results will be. It's just a wild guess because it's really incalculable. The numbers and the different ramifications are quite beyond linear computation. A worldwide pandemic is happening, and the economic repercussions will affect all of our ways of life, and this is again uncertainty.

People do become aware of the insecurity of life, like in the midst of wars and in the midst of economic collapses, all of these kinds of things. They're aware of it, but how do they respond to it? They respond with anxiety and terror and nightmares and shock, post-traumatic stress disorder, etc., but this is not how you should respond to it, because it's always the case.

Sometimes it's a little bit amplified, sometimes it's close to you. Now it seems you hear nothing else on the news but the number of cases and deaths from this pandemic, but it shouldn't produce any sense of anxiety or excessive concern whatsoever. Why? Because it's always the case that things are out of control. They always are, and you need to be fine in the midst of the chaos.

I have this saying: "Don't worry, everything is out of control." Once you really and truly get that, you will stop worrying, you will stop being fearful, because those negative feelings won't change the existential situation we are all in. Illness, aging, death, and loss are always with us. The uncertainty of how close we are to death is unknown to us. It can be an inch away at any time. There has never been even a single moment in history when human life has been safe and secure.

## Rehearsing for Death

Humans have this capacity of imagination; they can project into the future. One of the sayings is we're the only animal that knows they're going to die. We're aware of our mortality, but that's a problem. The advanced development of your prefrontal cortex lets you into a different universe than the other animals, but it also makes you aware of your mortality. The priority in life is to grapple with and understand this fact that you're not getting out alive, nobody is.

### *Log of Wood*

You will notice in Thailand that funerals are quite different than you might experience in the west. There you will find a calm acceptance of death. The monks chant a funeral *paritta*, a protection, which is basically a description of reality: here is a body; it is devoid of consciousness; it's like a log of wood on the ground. To us it may seem a weird funeral rite, more like a simple report: "Here's the body, no consciousness, nothing to see here, it's gone, consciousness moved on." It's very short, just a scientific description of what has happened. *Anicca vata sankhara*. Impermanent are all formations.

So how should you respond to the fact that you'll one day be just a log of wood? How should you feel about that? What is an intelligent emotional response to this? The Buddha says, well, by not wishing it was some other way or being shocked by it or not thinking about it. It's to see it clearly and understand what would be the best emotional response to this situation, and it is not suffering.

The proper response when reflecting on death is ease and non fear, no fear. Equanimity, loving-kindness, compassion, but no fear. There's not a time for fear and a time not for fear. It's always a time not for fear, because life is always dangerous.

## *Good Deeds from the Past*

It's slippery. I had to work on this myself for many, many years, to get the mind to acknowledge this and respond to it in a different way. You're not responding emotionally the same way. This is kind of a repetitive rehearsal that you need to do. And what should you be rehearsing? Positive events, looking back and revisiting your acts of generosity and kindness. Those should be played out again and again, especially as you approach the end of life.

The advice for those who are dying is do not dwell on your failings and negative past. It darkens your consciousness at a time when you really don't need any more darkness. The encouragement is to stay away from sadness, remorse, fear, all of those things, especially because you're dying.

You want to reshape your consciousness in the brightest way possible. You want to keep coming back to this sense of ease, of loving-kindness, of peace, again and again, and you fail at it, you get caught at times, you lose it, you can't remember it, but you need to repeat it all day and even into your sleep. You're not bringing up fear in the midst of this. Fear is simply not allowed.

## *Breath Meditation*

One of the hard truths about COVID-19 is that dying can be prolonged and uncomfortable. You're intubated and you can't breathe. You're drowning in the inability of your lungs to process the oxygen. They put a tube down your throat, which is very obnoxious and painful. Breathing itself becomes problematic. It's important that you actually practice this ahead of time. Practice being with the breath because it pulls you into the present. The breath will be with you until the end.

These days now, how they deal with people in the advanced stages of this disease is that they intubate them first, put some oxygen in there, but if they're continuing to go downhill, then they put them into a coma and they lose consciousness. So the last thing you'll ever experience is your own breath, and usually, in very many cases, you don't come out of that coma. That's the last thing, and you die.

However, if you have put lots of time into breath meditation, it's a very worthwhile investment. Your consciousness is collected, it's something that is there with you, you're not freaking out, and it can be very beneficial.

I talked to a woman who had learned to practice breath meditation just for a year or two. She ended up in the emergency room with some sort of constriction of her breath and swelling of the throat. Anaphylactic shock or something similar to that. The medical people were quite amazed at how calm she was. They often deal with anaphylactic panic, a panic response when you can't breathe. It can happen from a bee sting or an allergic reaction, and your throat closes up. She was recounting it to me, saying, "I was really just aware of the slowness, this little trickle of breath, and I was staying with it and staying with it. I was able to be lucid and calm because of having practiced so much with the breath."

Also there are different respiratory responses to panic. You'll see doctors looking at respiration and one of the features of a person in panic is their respirations per minute go up to 30 or 40, and one of the features of calmness is that the respirations go down. So a couple of the upsides of practicing breath meditation are calmness and the respirations per minute are reduced.

In the Buddhist commentaries they say that for one who cultivates breath meditation, one of the side-effects is you can anticipate your own death. That you have an intuition of the end of breathing, a knowing about when your death is coming, and that's one of the benefits of breath meditation.

There are some stories you find in the Visuddhimagga about monks predicting their own death. There's this particular story of a senior monk who had been practicing breath meditation. He said to the junior monks, "You know, you've heard of monks dying in meditation, in lotus meditation. Have you ever seen one die while walking? I want you to come to the terrace tomorrow in the afternoon. I will be doing walking meditation." The junior monks show up the next day and he's walking back and forth, and at the end of one of the walking lengths, just before he turns around, he dies. He knew he was going to die, and it was kind of his way of saying that dying while sitting is for amateurs. I can do it standing. I can do it walking.

Look at this breath and its relationship to death because it is the last thing. No breath, no life.

### *Maranasati: Mindfulness of Death Meditation*

Another suggestion as one approaches death is to practice the mindfulness exercise about the nature of death, *maranasati*, mindfulness of death or mindfulness of a corpse, contemplating a corpse, your own corpse, your own body.

The Buddha once asked a group of monks: "How do you do death meditation? How do you do *maranasati*, mindfulness of death?" One says, "I think to myself, 'I could die next week.'" Another says, "I could die tomorrow." The third monk says, "I could die at the end of this breath." And the Buddha says, "That's good enough."

It's not to bring up your fear around this; it's to contemplate this in serenity. When fear comes up, you know you're bringing the wrong emotion to this structure, so if that's the case then you can let that go. Come back to something like loving-kindness or breath meditation; calm the mind and then return again to the topic of mindfulness of death.

The idea of dying next week or tomorrow is not truly in touch with reality, but the end of this breath is close enough. It can happen before the end of this breath. All you have to do is have a heart attack or a stroke and you're done. It's that fast. If you're in a war, just a bullet through the head. That fast. Car accident? It's that fast.

## Grand Truths

We have to reflect on all of these aspects of life countless times throughout our days. And people respond to each of these aspects in a different way. Some people say, I don't mind dying, I just don't want the pain around it, or as Woody Allen says, "It's not that I'm afraid to die. I just don't want to be there when it happens."

For some, loss is worse than death, so they will choose death over loss. You see people, the famous and the obscure, jumping out of windows at The Wall Street Crash of the Great Depression in 1929. Executives and investors, losing their fortunes, and just jumping out of windows. Sheer madness! They were clearly more averse to loss than they were to death.

Some people just don't want to age. They want to live hard and leave a beautiful corpse. Notice how many of the rock stars have checked out at age 27? Everybody's got their thing, take your choice: illness, aging, death, and loss. Which one bothers you the most?

Actually all of these certainties are not intrinsically serious topics. It's the fear that goes with them, that's the serious topic. The Buddha is focused on the suffering, the psychological dimension of how we respond to this impossible situation. You can't get around this stuff. You only have one reasonable choice and that is to stop being afraid. That's the only sane response to this existence because you can't get out of these situations. They're not negotiable. You can try to negotiate, but you will not get anywhere except with this ultimate aim, which in Buddhism is *Nibbana*.

*Nibbana* is the deathless, the end of suffering, the cessation of suffering, right liberation. That's a good thing to have in mind as a possibility. It is a very exalted, difficult to understand concept, but we can get a taste of it. We're not always in fear, and when you're not in fear, when you're feeling balanced and peaceful, you probably like that. You think, "I'd like more of that. I'd like to be able to bring this into every situation."

This is not a place you want to continue on in, this *samsara*, this confused state of mind. *Samsara* is not a place, it's a condition of consciousness. The Buddha says, "Don't misunderstand this as some place you can find a satisfactory condition. Ultimately it is all unsatisfactory." We need to acknowledge this: illness, aging, death, and loss. We need to conduct ourselves in the midst of this *samsara*, this unsatisfactory situation, with great goodwill, generosity, and kindness; this minimizes the suffering content of it.

At the same time, we have to retain the ultimate vision that we need to completely free ourselves and not return. This is the final stage of maturity: "Been there, done that." We have addictive tendencies and the addictive tendencies are based on delusions. We forget and we go back. You can see this in profound addiction, why people keep returning to very unskillful ways. They simply can't remember the downside of their delusion.

# LIFE IS A NEAR DEATH EXPERIENCE

Basically all of *samsara* and the tendency to take birth over and over again is a forgetfulness of the downside, which is how it ends. It's a matter of loss, you lose in the end, and that, from a Buddhist point of view, is summed up in the Dhammapada: "Even in heaven it ends in tears."[5]

Now, we're from a Judeo Christian society where heaven is often described as an eternal condition of bliss or peace or safety. It can be quite disturbing to the Christian and post-Christian mind to come across this premise that heaven is a very long period of time of well-being, but that it comes to an end.

This is quite upsetting, and people can very strongly reject that idea. It's stuff you don't want to hear. It's actually quite a thing to face: the truth, the Dhamma, about the intrinsic flaw in existence. It's built into all existence, that's why existence is problematic.

This is a very elevated idea. Maybe you've never really heard Dhamma or Buddhism. You might be a meditator, perhaps you've gone to a mindfulness course or a loving-kindness course, but you really haven't been exposed to the larger perspectives of Buddhism, of the Dhamma. You might even find this rather unsettling. However, I'm a Buddhist monk living in a Buddhist monastery, and if I don't talk about these ultimate things

---

[5] Dhammapada v. 186

here, where do you talk about them?

In the West, Buddhism seems to be a popular alternative to many of the other religions and philosophies. One reason is because it's intrinsically peaceful; there's no violent admonition in it. Also there's a lot of psychology to it, so you get to meditate and escape the world for a while. Who can complain about loving-kindness or mindfulness or such tranquil things? But quite often the larger view of reality is not well known. Those who teach these courses of mindfulness and loving-kindness know their audience quite well. They know that the general population is really often not there to hear grand truths. They're actually there for some therapy to get them through the next two weeks, or the next year, or to improve the emotional quality of their life.

Which it does. But it's a disservice to the Buddha and the Dhamma and the Sangha to not tell people about the larger dimensions of what the Buddha really taught. There's a time and place for it. It's not something you blurt out on the street corner. The Buddha had discretion. He looked at the person he was talking to and he recognized that for certain people it's not the time and place to talk about these big issues. This is the time and place for just some practical advice.

He's not wanting to shock people. He's always

interested in beneficial speech: it's got to be true, but it's got to be beneficial at the same time. If you say things that a person is not ready to hear, it will not be beneficial. It may be true, but it won't be beneficial. There's a certain amount of skill in this as well. But the larger truths are there, and we're in the midst of this pandemic, so we have to face illness, aging, death, and loss. Again and again and again. That's the big picture.

## *Your Constant Companion*

There was a man I met many years ago who had been a carpenter when they were building the original structures at Arrow River. This was before it became the hermitage. He had fallen off one of the roofs of the building he was working on and broke his neck and was now a quadriplegic for life. I had never met him before, but Ajahn Punnadhammo and I went to visit him in his care facility.

I asked him if he meditated and he said, "Yes, I meditate. Every day. You see the reason I fell off that roof was because I was still drunk from the night before. I was an alcoholic, heading towards death, and only this fall saved my life. I am so grateful."

Sometimes it takes a dramatic shift in life to set us on the spiritual path. It could be a severe accident or a terminal illness, losing your job or your loved ones. It could be the dramatic shifts in societies and cultures that we've witnessed during this pandemic, or the impact of climate change that continues to bear down on us, just like those mountains as high as the Himalayas. Yet through it all we have a choice.

We can reflect on these choices with our mind, with our imagination, with our heart. We just have to choose with a relaxed stomach and not with fear or any of these types of emotions. Only then can we allow ourselves to go into the facts of life with serenity. "I know these are the real possibilities. I need to practice my emotional response to this now. I need to be calm."

You can't freak out, you can't lose your mind. That's the worst thing you can do in this dire situation we call life. These are just the facts. We're always at war with the facts of life. Illness, aging, death, and loss are always a constant companion. The Buddha says, "This is your constant companion, death, *maranasati*."

---

I'll leave you now with one of the Ten Subjects for Frequent Reflection the Buddha gave to monks and nuns[6]. It's something all of us can reflect upon: "The days and nights are relentlessly passing; how well am I spending my time?"

---

[6] AN 10:48: Pabbajitaabhinhasutta (Ten Subjects for Frequent Reflection by One Who Has Gone Forth)

## Handful of Teachings: Part II

***The Buddha and The King:*** Practice the reflections of illness, aging, death, and loss until they are running in the background of your mind every waking moment, and into your dreams. Your duty, in the face of these vicissitudes, is to always be virtuous and to always do good deeds. Just these will serve you well all the days of your life.

***Don't Worry, Everything is Out of Control:*** Nothing in life is safe. Nothing is secure. Once you really know this truth, you will stop worrying, you will stop being fearful. The Buddhist response is to be at ease with all of this. "Know that the body is a fragile jar, and make a castle of your mind."

***Rehearsing for Death:*** Bring to mind your past good deeds, your acts of generosity and kindness. Practice breath meditation and *maranasati,* mindfulness of death meditation. The idea of dying next week or tomorrow is not truly in touch with reality, but the end of this breath is close enough. Any time, and especially at the end of life, is no time for fear.

***Grand Truths:*** The Buddha taught just two things: suffering and its end. *Samsara*, this confused state of mind, is suffering, and not a place you want to continue on in. *Nibbana* is the deathless, the end of suffering, right liberation. That's the ultimate grand truth and the ultimate goal of Buddhism.

***Your Constant Companion:*** Sometimes it takes a dramatic shift in our lives to set us on the spiritual path. Through it all we have a choice. The Buddha asks us to choose calm and ease in the face of fear and delusion. "The days and nights are relentlessly passing; how well am I spending my time?"

# REFERENCES/GLOSSARY

## *References*

| | |
|---|---|
| Anguttara Nikaya (AN) | Numerical Discourses |
| Dhammapada (DHP) | Verses on Dhamma |
| Khuddaka Patha (KP) | Minor Readings |
| Visuddhimagga | Path of Purification |

## *Glossary: Pali/English*

| Pali | English |
|---|---|
| *Anicca* | Impermanence |
| *Bhikkhu* | Buddhist monk |
| *Buddha* | Self-awakened enlightened being |
| *Dhamma* | A Buddha's teachings |
| *Jhana, Samedhi* | Meditation, stilling the mind |
| *Kamma* | Intentional actions |
| *Maranasati* | Mindfulness of death |
| *Metta* | Loving-kindness |
| *Nibbana* | Final deliverance from suffering |
| *Paramis* | Perfections of character |
| *Paritta* | Chant of protection |
| *Samsara* | Round of unsatisfactory existence |
| *Sankhara* | Formations, volitions |
| *Sangha* | Monastic community, monks, nuns |
| *Sati* | Mindfulness |
| *Sutta* | Discourse |

## ABOUT THE AUTHOR

Ajahn Sona is the Abbot of Birken Forest Buddhist Monastery (Pali name: 'Sitavana') located in British Columbia, Canada, and the author of *Bloom: Buddhist Reflections on Serenity and Love.*

Made in the USA
Middletown, DE
03 June 2024